Human Language Technologies: The 2010 Annual Conference of the North American Chapter of the Association for Computational Linguistics (NAACL HLT 2010)

Tutorial Abstracts

Los Angeles, California, USA
1 June 2010

ISBN: 978-1-61738-706-7

Printed from e-media with permission by:

Curran Associates, Inc.
57 Morehouse Lane
Red Hook, NY 12571

Some format issues inherent in the e-media version may also appear in this print version.

Printed by Curran Associates, Inc. (2010)

For permission requests, please contact the Association for Computational Linguistics
at the address below.

Association for Computational Linguistics
209 N. Eighth Street
Stroudsburg, Pennsylvania 18360

Phone: 1-570-476-8006
Fax: 1-570-476-0860

acl@aclweb.org

Additional copies of this publication are available from:

Curran Associates, Inc.
57 Morehouse Lane
Red Hook, NY 12571 USA
Phone: 845-758-0400
Fax: 845-758-2634
Email: curran@proceedings.com
Web: www.proceedings.com

NAACL HLT 2010

Human Language Technologies: The 2010 Annual Conference of the North American Chapter of the Association for Computational Linguistics

Tutorial Abstracts

Jason Baldridge, Peter Clark, Gokhan Tur
Tutorial Chairs

June 1, 2010
Los Angeles, California

Table of Contents

Conference Program

Tuesday, June 1, 2010

Morning

Data-Intensive Text Processing with MapReduce
Jimmy Lin and Chris Dyer

Markov Logic in Natural Language Processing: Theory, Algorithms, and Applications
Hoifung Poon

Noisy Text Analytics
L. Venkata Subramaniam

Recent Advances in Dependency Parsing
Qin Iris Wang and Yue Zhang

Afternoon

Integer Linear Programming in NLP - Constrained Conditional Models
Ming-Wei Wang, Nicholas Rizzolo and Dan Roth

Distributional Semantic Models
Stefan Evert

Computational psycholinguistics
Roger Levy, Klinton Bicknell and Nathaniel Smith

Textual Entailment
Mark Sammons, Idan Szpektor and V.G.Vinod Vydiswaran

Data-Intensive Text Processing with MapReduce

Jimmy Lin and Chris Dyer
University of Maryland, College Park
{jimmylin,redpony}@umd.edu

1. Overview

This half-day tutorial introduces participants to data-intensive text processing with the MapReduce programming model [1], using the open-source Hadoop implementation. The focus will be on scalability and the tradeoffs associated with distributed processing of large datasets. Content will include general discussions about algorithm design, presentation of illustrative algorithms, case studies in HLT applications, as well as practical advice in writing Hadoop programs and running Hadoop clusters.

2. Intended Audience

The tutorial is targeted at any NLP researcher who is interested in data-intensive processing and scalability issues in general. No background in parallel or distributed computing is necessary, but a prior knowledge of HLT is assumed.

3. Course Objectives

* Acquire understanding of the MapReduce programming model and how it relates to alternative approaches to concurrent programming.

* Acquire understanding of how data-intensive HLT problems (e.g., text retrieval, iterative optimization problems, and graph algorithms) can be solved using MapReduce.

* Acquire understanding of the tradeoffs involved in designing MapReduce algorithms and awareness of associated engineering issues.

4. Tutorial Topics

The following represents a tentative list of topics that will be covered:

* Introduction to parallel and distributed processing
* Introduction to MapReduce
* Tradeoffs and issues in algorithm design
* Simple counting applications (e.g., relative frequency estimation)
* Applications to inverted indexing and text retrieval
* Applications to graph algorithms

* Applications to iterative optimization algorithms (e.g., EM)
* Case study in machine translation
* Tips and tricks in writing Hadoop programs
* Practical issues in running Hadoop clusters

5. Instructor Bios

Jimmy Lin is an Associate Professor in the iSchool at the University of Maryland, College Park. He joined the faculty in 2004 after completing his Ph.D. in Electrical Engineering and Computer Science at MIT. Dr Lin's research interests lie at the intersection of natural language processing and information retrieval. He leads the University of Maryland's effort in the Google/IBM Academic Cloud Computing Initiative. Dr. Lin has taught two semester-long Hadoop courses and has given numerous talks and tutorials about MapReduce to a wide audience.

Chris Dyer is a Ph.D. student at the University of Maryland, College Park, in the Department of Linguistics. His current research interests include statistical machine translation, machine learning, and the relationship between artificial language processing systems and the human linguistic processing system. He has served on program committees for AMTA, ACL, COLING, EACL, EMNLP, NAACL, ISWLT, and the ACL Workshops on Machine translation, and is one of the developers of the Moses open source machine translation toolkit. He has practical experience solving NLP problems with both the Hadoop MapReduce framework and Google's MapReduce implementation, which was made possible by an internship with Google Research in 2008.

References

[1] Dean, Jeffrey and Sanjay Ghemawat. MapReduce: Simplified Data Processing on Large Clusters. Proceedings of the 6th Symposium on Operating System Design and Implementation (OSDI 2004), p. 137-150, 2004, San Francisco, California.

[2] Jimmy Lin. Exploring Large-Data Issues in the Curriculum: A Case Study with MapReduce. Proceedings of the Third Workshop on Issues in Teaching Computational Linguistics (TeachCL-08) at ACL 2008, p. 54-61, 2008, Columbus, Ohio.

Markov Logic in Natural Language Processing: Theory, Algorithms, and Applications

Hoifung Poon, University of Washington

Natural languages are characterized by rich relational structures and tight integration with world knowledge. As the field of NLP/CL moves towards more complex and challenging tasks, there has been increasing interest in applying joint inference to leverage such relations and prior knowledge. Recent work in statistical relational learning (a.k.a. structured prediction) has shown that joint inference can not only substantially improve predictive accuracy, but also enable effective learning with little or no labeled information. Markov logic is the unifying framework for statistical relational learning, and has spawned a series of successful NLP applications, ranging from information extraction to unsupervised semantic parsing. In this tutorial, I will introduce Markov logic to the NLP community and survey existing NLP applications. The target audience of the tutorial is all NLP researchers, students and practitioners. The audience will gain the ability to efficiently develop state-of-the-art solutions to NLP problems using Markov logic and the Alchemy open-source software.

1. Structure

The tutorial will be structured as follows:

Part One: Markov Logic

In the first part I will motivate statistical relational learning (SRL) for NLP problems, and introduce Markov logic as the unifying framework. I will present state-of-the-art learning and inference algorithms in Markov logic, and give an overview of the Alchemy open-source software package. The duration of this part will be approximately one hour and half.

Part Two: NLP Applications: Supervised Learning

In the second part I will describe how to use Markov logic and Alchemy to develop state-of-the-art solutions very efficiently for a variety of NLP problems, including: logistic regression, text and hypertext classification, vector-space and link-based information retrieval, entity resolution, information integration, hidden Markov models, Bayesian networks, information extraction, semantic role labeling, and biomedical text mining. This part will also cover practical tips on using Markov logic and Alchemy — the kind of information that is rarely found in research papers, but is key to developing successful applications. This part will focus on supervised learning and the duration will be approximately an hour.

Part Three: NLP Applications: Unsupervised Learning

In the third and final part I will introduce the emerging direction for statistical relation learning that leverages prior knowledge and relational structures to enable effective learning with little or no labeled data. As examples I will present recent work in applying Markov logic to unsupervised coreference resolution and unsupervised semantic parsing. I will also briefly touch on the exciting prospect of machine reading from the Web. The duration will be about half an hour.

2. Instructor

Hoifung Poon

Department of Computer Science and Engineering
University of Washington
Seattle, WA 98195, USA
hoifung@cs.washington.edu

Hoifung Poon is a fifth-year Ph.D. student at the University of Washington, working with Pedro Domingos. His main research interest lies in advancing machine learning methods to handle both complexity and uncertainty, and in applying them to solving challenging NLP problems with little or no labeled data. His most recent work developed unsupervised learning methods for a number of NLP problems ranging from morphological segmentation to semantic parsing, and received the Best Paper Awards in NAACL-09 and EMNLP-09. At Washington, he helped design course materials for the first offering of the undergraduate machine learning course, and gave guest lectures in both undergraduate and graduate machine learning classes. His prior experience includes teaching undergraduate math classes in West Virginia University, for which he was awarded the Outstanding Graduate Teaching Assistant by the University.

Noisy Text Analytics

L. Venkata Subramaniam, IBM Research India

Text produced in informal settings (email, blogs, tweet, SMS, chat) and text which results from processing (speech recognition, OCR, machine translation, historical text) is inherently noisy. This tutorial will cover the efforts of the computational linguistics community in moving beyond traditional techniques to contend with the noise.

1. Overview

Text produced by processing signals intended for human use is often noisy for automated computer processing. Digital text produced in informal settings such as online chat, SMS, emails, tweets, message boards, newsgroups, blogs, wikis and web pages contain considerable noise. Also processing techniques like Automatic Speech Recognition, Optical Character Recognition and Machine Translation introduce processing noise. People are adept when it comes to pattern recognition tasks involving typeset or handwritten documents or recorded speech, machines less-so.

Noise can manifest itself at the earliest stages of processing in the form of degraded inputs that our systems must be prepared to handle. Many downstream applications use techniques meant for clean text. It is only recently that with the increase in noisy text, these techniques are being adapted to handle noisy text. This tutorial will focus on the problems encountered in analyzing such noisy text coming from various sources. Noise introduces challenges that need special handling, either through new methods or improved versions of existing ones. For example, missing punctuation and the use of non-standard words can often hinder standard natural language processing techniques such as part-of-speech tagging and parsing. Further downstream applications such as Information Retrieval, Information Extraction and Text mining have to explicitly handle noise in order to return useful results. Often, depending on the application, the noise can be modeled and it may be possible to develop specific strategies to immunize the system from the effects of noise and improve performance. This tutorial will cover:

* Various sources of noise and their characteristics as well as typical metrics used to measure noise.
* Methods to handle noise by moving beyond traditional natural language processing techniques.
* Methods to overcome noise in specific applications like IR, IE, QA, MT, etc.

2. Outline

The tutorial will have three parts:

* What is Noise
    - o Detecting Noise

    o Classifying Noise
    o Quantifying Noise

* Processing and/or Correcting Noise
    o Spelling Correction
    o Natural Language Processing of Noisy Text: Segmentation, Parsing, POS
    o Learning underlying language models in presence of noise

* Effect of Noise on Downstream Applications
    o Information Retrieval from Noisy Text
    o Information Extraction from Noisy Text
    o Classification of Noisy Text
    o Summarization of Noisy Text
    o Machine Translation of Noisy Text

3. Target Audience

This tutorial is designed for students and researchers in Computer Science and Computational Linguistics. Elementary knowledge of text processing is assumed. This topic is expected to be of wide interest given its relevance to the computational linguistics community. Since noisy data is also the main theme of NAACL HLT 2010, good audience participation can be expected.

4. Speaker's Bio

L Venkata Subramaniam manages the information processing and analytics group at IBM Research – India. He received his PhD from IIT Delhi in 1999. His research focuses on unstructured information management, statistical natural language processing, noisy text analytics, text and data mining, information theory, speech and image processing. He often teaches and guides student thesis at IIT Delhi on these topics. He co founded the AND (Analytics for Noisy Unstructured Text Data) workshop series and also co-chaired the first three workshops, 2007-2009. He was guest co-editor of two special issues on Noisy Text Analytics in the International Journal of Document Analysis and Recognition in 2007 and 2009.

Recent Advances in Dependency Parsing

Qin Iris Wang, AT&T Interactive
Yue Zhang, Oxford

Data-driven (statistical) approaches have been playing an increasingly prominent role in parsing since the 1990s. In recent years, there has been a growing interest in dependency-based as opposed to constituency-based approaches to syntactic parsing, with application to a wide range of research areas and different languages. Graph-based and transition-based methods are the two dominant data-driven approaches to dependency parsing. In a graph-based model, it defines a space of candidate dependency trees for a given sentence. Each candidate tree is scored via a local or global scoring function. The parser (usually uses dynamic programming) outputs the highest-scored tree. In contrast, in a transition-based model, it defines a transition system for mapping a sentence to its dependency tree. It induces a model for predicting the next state transition, given the transition history. Given the induced model, the output parse tree is built deterministically upon the construction of the optimal transition sequence.

Both Graph-based and transition-based approaches have been used to achieve state-of-the-art dependency parsing results for a wide range of languages. Some researchers have used the combination of the two models and it shows the performance of the combined model is significantly better than the individual models. Another recent trend is to apply online training to shift-reduce parsing in the transition-based models. In this tutorial, we first introduce the two main-stream data-driven dependency parsing models--- graph-based and transition-based models. After comparing the differences between them, we show how these two models can be combined in various ways to achieve better results.

Outline

Part A: Introduction to Dependency Parsing

Part B: Graph-based Dependency Parsing Models

- Learning Algorithms (Local Learning vs. Global Learning)
- Parsing Algorithms (Dynamic Programming)
- Features (Static Features vs. Dynamic Features)

Part C: Transition-based Dependency Parsing Models

- Learning Algorithms (Local Learning vs. online Learning)
- Parsing Algorithms (Shift-reduce Parsing)
- Features

Part D: The Combined Models

- The stacking Method
- The ensemble Method
- Single-model Combination

Part E: Other Recent Trends in Dependency Parsing
- Integer Linear Programming
- Fast Non-Projective Parsing

Presenters

Qin Iris Wang
Email: qiniriswang@gmail.com

Qin Iris Wang is currently a Research Scientist at AT&T Interactive (San Francisco). Qin obtained her PhD in 2008 from the University of Alberta under Dekang Lin and Dale Schuurmans. Qin's research interests include NLP (in particular dependency parsing), machine learning, information retrieval, text mining and large scale data processing. Qin's PhD studies was focused on Learning Structured Classifiers for Statistical Dependency Parsing. Before joined AT&T, she was a research scientist at Yahoo Labs. Qin was a teaching assistant for two years during her PhD studies. In 2009, Qin organized a workshop on " Semi-supervised Learning for Natural Language Processing" at NAACL-HLT.

Yue Zhang
Email: yue.zhang@comlab.ox.ac.uk

Yue Zhang just defended his PhD thesis at the University of Oxford. Yue's research interests include natural language processing (word segmentation, parsing, machine translation), machine learning, etc. More specifically, his research area is the syntactic analysis of the Chinese language, using discriminative machine-learning approaches. He has worked on word segmentation, joint word segmentation and POS-tagging, phrase-structure parsing and dependency parsing. Yue worked on Chinese-English machine-translation during MSc studies in Oxford, and parallel computing during undergrad studies in Tsinghua University.

Integer Linear Programming in NLP - Constrained Conditional Models

Ming-Wei Chang, Nicholas Rizzolo, Dan Roth
University of Illinois at Urbana-Champaign

Making decisions in natural language processing problems often involves assigning values to sets of interdependent variables where the expressive dependency structure can influence, or even dictate, what assignments are possible. Structured learning problems such as semantic role labeling provide one such example, but the setting is broader and includes a range of problems such as name entity and relation recognition and co-reference resolution. The setting is also appropriate for cases that may require a solution to make use of multiple (possible pre-designed or pre-learned components) as in summarization, textual entailment and question answering. In all these cases, it is natural to formulate the decision problem as a constrained optimization problem, with an objective function that is composed of learned models, subject to domain or problem specific constraints.

Constrained Conditional Models (aka Integer Linear Programming formulation of NLP problems) is a learning and inference framework that augments the learning of conditional (probabilistic or discriminative) models with declarative constraints (written, for example, using a first-order representation) as a way to support decisions in an expressive output space while maintaining modularity and tractability of training and inference. In most applications of this framework in NLP, following [Roth & Yih, CoNLL'04], Integer Linear Programming (ILP) was used as the inference framework, although other algorithms can be used for that purpose.

This framework, with and without Integer Linear Programming as its inference engine, has recently attracted much attention within the NLP community, with multiple papers in all the recent major conferences, and a related workshop in NAACL'09. Formulating problems as constrained optimization problems over the output of learned models has several advantages. It allows one to focus on the modeling of problems by providing the opportunity to incorporate problem specific global constraints using a first order language – thus frees the developer from (much of the) low level feature engineering – and it guarantees exact inference. It provides also the freedom of decoupling the stage of model generation (learning) from that of the constrained inference stage, often resulting in simplifying the learning stage as well as the engineering problem of building an NLP system, while improving the quality of the solutions.

These advantages and the availability of off-the-shelf solvers have led to a large variety of natural language processing tasks being formulated within framework, including semantic role labeling, syntactic parsing, coreference resolution, summarization, transliteration and joint information extraction.

The goal of this tutorial is to introduce the framework of Constrained Conditional Models (CCMs) to the broader ACL community, motivate it as a generic framework for learning and inference in global NLP decision problems, present some of the key theoretical and practical issues involved in using CCMs and survey some of the existing applications of it as a way to promote further development of the framework and additional applications. The tutorial will thus be useful for many of the senior and junior researchers that have interest in global decision problems in NLP, providing a concise overview of recent perspectives and research results.

Tutorial Outline

After shortly motivating and introducing the general framework, the main part of the tutorial is a methodological presentation of some of the key computational issues studied within CCMs that we will present by looking at case studies published in the NLP literature. In the last part of the tutorial, we will discuss engineering issues that arise in using CCMs and present some tool that facilitate developing CCM models.

1. Motivation and Task Definition [30 min]

We will motivate the framework of Constrained Conditional Models and exemplify it using the example of Semantic Role Labeling.

2. Examples of Existing Applications [30 min]

We will present in details several applications that made use of CCMs – including coreference resolution, sentence compression and information extraction and use these to explain several of the key advantages the framework offers. We will discuss in this context several ways in which constraints can be introduced to an application.

3. Training Paradigms [30 min]

The objective function used by CCMs can be decomposed and learned in several ways, ranging from a complete joint training of the model along with the constraints to a complete decoupling between the learning and the inference stage. We will present the advantages and disadvantages offered by different training paradigms and provide theoretical and experimental understanding. In this part we will also discuss comparison to other approaches studied in the literature.

4. Inference methods and Constraints [30 min]

We will present and discuss several possibilities for modeling inference in CCMs, from Integer Linear Programming to search techniques. We will also discuss the use of hard constraints and soft constraints and present ways for modeling constraints.

5. Introducing background knowledge via CCMs [30 min]

We will look at ways in which Constrained Conditional Models (CCMs)can be used to augment probabilistic models with declarative constraints in order to support decisions in an expressive output space, and how declarative constraints can be used to aid supervised and semi-supervised training.

6. Developing CCMs Applications [30 min]

We present a modeling language that facilitates developing applications within the CCM framework and present some “templates” for possible applications.

Tutorial Instructors

Ming-Wei Chang

Computer Science Department, University of Illinois at Urbana-Champaign, IL, 61801

Email: mchang21@uiuc.edu

Ming-Wei Chang is a Phd candidate in University of Illinois at Urbana-Champaign.

He has done work on Machine Learning in Natural Language Processing and Information Extraction and has published a number of papers in several international conferences including "Learning and Inference with Constraints" (AAAI'08), "Guiding Semi-Supervision with Constraint-Driven Learning" (ACL'07) and “Unsupervised Constraint Driven Learning For Transliteration Discovery. (NAACL'09). He co-presented a tutorial on CCMs in EACL'09.

Nicholas Rizzolo

Computer Science Department, University of Illinois at Urbana-Champaign, IL, 61801

Email: ratinov2@uiuc.edu

Nicholas Rizollo is a Phd candidate in University of Illinois at Urbana-Champaign.

He has done work on Machine Learning in Natural Language Processing and is the principal developer of Learning Based Java (LBJ) a modeling language for Constrained Conditional Models. He has published a number of papers on these topics, including "Learning and Inference with Constraints" (AAAI'08) and “Modeling Discriminative Global Inference” (ICSC'07)

Dan Roth

Computer Science Department, University of Illinois at Urbana-Champaign, IL, 61801

Phone: +(217) 244-7068; Email: danr@cs.uiuc.edu

Dan Roth is a Professor in the Department of Computer Science at the University of Illinois at Urbana-Champaign and the Beckman Institute of Advanced Science and Technology (UIUC) and a Willett Faculty Scholar of the College of Engineering. He has published broadly in machine learning, natural language processing, knowledge representation and reasoning and received several best paper and research awards. He has developed several machine learning based natural language processing systems including an award winning semantic parser, and has presented invited talks in several international conferences, and several tutorials on machine learning for NLP. Dan Roth has written the first paper on Constrained Conditional Models along with his student Scott Yih, presented in CoNLL'04, and since then has worked on learning and inference issue within this framework as well as on applying it for several NLP problems, including Semantic Role Labeling, Information Extraction and Transliteration. He has presented several invited talks that have addresses aspect of this model.

Bibliography

Dan Roth and Wen-tau Yih. A Linear Programming Formulation for Global Inference in Natural Language Tasks. In Proceedings of the Eighth Conference on Computational Natural Language Learning (CoNLL-2004), pages 1-8, 2004.

Vasin Punyakanok, Dan Roth, Wen-tau Yih, and Dav Zimak. Semantic Role Labeling Via Integer Linear Programming Inference. In Proceedings of the International Conference on Computational Linguistics (COLING-2004), pages 1346-1352, 2004.)

Tomacz Marciniak and Michael Strube. Beyond the Pipeline: Discrete Optimization in NLP. In Proceedings of the Ninth Conference on Computational Natural Language Learning (CoNLL-2005), pages 136-145, 2005.

Tzong-Han Tsai, Chia-Wei Wu, Yu-Chun Lin, and Wen-Lian Hsu. Exploiting Full Parsing Information to Label Semantic Roles Using an Ensemble of ME and SVM via Integer Linear Programming. In Proceedings of the Ninth Conference on Computational Natural Language Learning: Shared Task (CoNLL-2005) Shared Task, pages 233-236, 2005.

Vasin Punyakanok, Dan Roth and Wen-tau Yih. The Necessity of Syntactic Parsing for Semantic Role Labeling. In Proceedings of the International Joint Conference on Artificial Intelligence (IJCAI-2005), pages 1117-1123, 2005.

Vasin Punyakanok, Dan Roth, Wen-tau Yih and Dav Zimak. Learning and Inference over Constrained Output. In Proceedings of the International Joint Conference on Artificial Intelligence (IJCAI-2005), pages 1124-1129, 2005.

Dan Roth and Wen-tau Yih. Integer Linear Programming Inference for Conditional Random Fields. In Proceedings of the International Conference on Machine Learning (ICML-2005), pages 737-744, 2005.

Regina Barzilay and Mirella Lapata. Aggregation via Set Partitioning for Natural Language Generation. In Proceedings of the Human Language Technology Conference of the North American Chapter of the Association of Computational Linguistics (HLT-NAACL-2006), pages 359-366, 2006.

James Clarke and Mirella Lapata. Constraint-Based Sentence Compression: An Integer Programming Approach. In Proceedings of the COLING/ACL 2006 Main Conference Poster Sessions (ACL-2006), pages 144-151, 2006.

Sebastian Riedel and James Clarke. Incremental Integer Linear Programming for Non-projective Dependency Parsing. In Proceedings of the 2006 Conference on Empirical Methods in Natural Language Processing (EMNLP-2006), pages 129-137, 2006.

Philip Bramsen, Pawan Deshpande, Yoong Keok Lee, and Regina Barzilay. Inducing Temporal Graphs. In Proceedings of the 2006 Conference on Empirical Methods in Natural Language Processing (EMNLP-2006), 189-198, 2006.

Yejin Choi, Eric Breck, and Claire Cardie. Joint Extraction of Entities and Relations for Opinion Recognition. In Proceedings of the 2006 Conference on Empirical Methods in Natural Language Processing (EMNLP-2006), 431-439, 2006.

Manfred Klenner. Grammatical Role Labeling with Integer Linear Programming. In Proceedings of the 11th Conference of the European Chapter of the Association for Computational Linguistics, Conference Companion (EACL-2006), pages 187-190, 2006.

Pascal Denis and Jason Baldridge. Joint Determination of Anaphoricity and Coreference Resolution using Integer Programming. In Proceedings of the Annual Meeting of the North American Chapter of the Association for Computational Linguistics - Human Language Technology Conference (NAACL-HLT-2007), pages 236-243, 2007.

James Clarke and Mirella Lapata. Modelling Compression with Discourse Constraints. In Proceedings of the Conference on Empirical Methods in Natural Language Processing and on Computational Natural Language Learning (EMNLP-CoNLL-2007), pages 1-11, 2007.

Manfred Klenner. Enforcing Consistency on Coreference Sets. In Recent Advances in Natural Language Processing (RANLP), pages 323-328, 2007

Dan Roth and Wen-tau Yih. Global Inference for Entity and Relation Identification via a Linear Programming Formulation. Introduction to Statistical Relational Learning, 2007.

K. Ganchev, João Graça and B. Taskar. Expectation Maximization and Posterior Constraints, Neural Information Processing Systems Conference (NIPS), Vancouver, BC, December 2007.

James Clarke and Mirella Lapata. Global Inference for Sentence Compression: An Integer Linear Programming Approach. Journal of Artificial Intelligence Research (JAIR), 31, pages 399-429, 2008.

Vasin Punyakanok, Dan Roth and Wen-tau Yih. The Importance of Syntactic Parsing and Inference in Semantic Role Labeling. Computational Linguistics 34(2), pages 257-287, 2008.

Jenny Rose Finkel and Christopher D. Manning. Enforcing Transitivity in Coreference Resolution. In Proceedings of the Annual Meeting of the Association for Computational Linguistics - Human Language Technology Conference, Short Papers (ACL-HLT-2008), pages 45-48, 2008.

K. Ganchev, João Graça and B. Taskar. Better Alignments = Better Translations?, Association for Computational Linguistics (ACL), Columbus, Ohio, June 2008.

Hal Daumé. Cross-Task Knowledge-Constrained Self Training In Proceedings of the 2008 Conference on Empirical Methods in Natural Language Processing (EMNLP-2008).

Dan Goldwasser and Dan Roth. Transliteration as Constrained Optimization. In Proceedings of the 2008 Conference on Empirical Methods in Natural Language Processing (EMNLP-2008), pages 353-362, 2008.

Distributional Semantic Models

Stefan Evert, University of Osnabrück

1. DESCRIPTION

Distributional semantic models (DSM) -- also known as "word space" or "distributional similarity" models -- are based on the assumption that the meaning of a word can (at least to a certain extent) be inferred from its usage, i.e. its distribution in text. Therefore, these models dynamically build semantic representations -- in the form of high-dimensional vector spaces -- through a statistical analysis of the contexts in which words occur. DSMs are a promising technique for solving the lexical acquisition bottleneck by unsupervised learning, and their distributed representation provides a cognitively plausible, robust and flexible architecture for the organisation and processing of semantic information.

Since the seminal papers of Landauer & Dumais (1997) and Schütze (1998), DSMs have been an active area of research in computational linguistics. Amongst many other tasks, they have been applied to solving the TOEFL synonym test (Landauer & Dumais 1997, Rapp 2004), automatic thesaurus construction (Lin 1998), identification of translation equivalents (Rapp 1999), word sense induction and discrimination (Schütze 1998), POS induction (Schütze 1995), identification of analogical relations (Turney 2006), PP attachment disambiguation (Pantel & Lin 2000), semantic classification (Versley 2008), as well as the prediction of fMRI (Mitchell et al. 2008) and EEG (Murphy et al. 2009) data. Recent years have seen renewed and rapidly growing interest in distributional approaches, as shown by the series of workshops on DSM held at Context 2007 [1], ESSLLI 2008 [2], EACL 2009 [3], CogSci 2009 [4], NAACL-HLT 2010 [5], ACL 2010 [6] and ESSLLI 2010 [7].

The proposed tutorial aims to
- introduce the most common DSM architectures and their parameters, as well as prototypical applications;
- equip participants with the mathematical techniques needed for the implementation of DSMs, in particular those of matrix algebra;
- illustrate visualisation techniques and mathematical arguments that help in understanding the high-dimensional DSM vector spaces and making sense of key operations such as SVD dimensionality reduction; and
- provide an overview of current research on DSMs, available software, evaluation tasks and future trends.

The tutorial is targeted both at participants who are new to the field and need a comprehensive overview of DSM techniques and applications, and at experienced scientists who want to get up to speed on current directions in DSM research.

An implementation of all methods presented in the tutorial will be provided as supplementary material, using the open-source statistical programming language R [8]. This implementation, which is based on the code and data sets available at [9], is intended as a "toy laboratory" for participants, but can also form a sound basis for practical applications and further DSM research.

2. TUTORIAL OUTLINE

1) Introduction
   - motivation and brief history of distributional semantics
   - common DSM architectures
   - prototypical applications
   - concrete examples used in the tutorial

2) Taxonomy of DSM parameters including
   - size and type of context window
   - feature scaling (tf.idf, statistical association measures, ...)
   - normalisation and standardisation of rows and/or columns
   - distance/similarity measures: Euclidean, Minkowski p-norms, cosine, entropy-based, ...
   - dimensionality reduction: feature selection, SVD, random indexing (RI)

3) Elements of matrix algebra for DSM
   - basic matrix and vector operations
   - norms and distances, angles, orthogonality
   - projection and dimensionality reduction

4) Making sense of DSMs: mathematical analysis and visualisation techniques
   - nearest neighbours and clustering
   - semantic maps: PCA, MDS, SOM
   - visualisation of high-dimensional spaces
   - supervised classification based on DSM vectors
   - understanding dimensionality reduction with SVD and RI
   - term-term vs. term-context matrix, connection to first-order association
   - SVD as a latent class model

5) Current research topics and future directions
   - overview of current research on DSMs
   - evaluation tasks and data sets
   - available "off-the-shelf" DSM software
   - limitations and key problems of DSMs
   - trends for future work

Each of the five parts will be compressed into a slot of roughly 30 minutes, leaving a 30-minute coffee break. In order to cover the large amount of material in a relatively short time, the discussion of mathematical and implementational aspects will aim primarily at an intuitive understanding of key issues and skip technical details. Full descriptions are provided as part of the handouts and supplementary material, esp. the thoroughly commented R implementation.

3. INSTRUCTOR

Stefan Evert
Juniorprofessor of Computational Linguistics
University of Osnabrück, Germany

Stefan Evert has studied mathematics, physics and English linguistics, and holds a PhD degree in computational linguistics. His research interests include the statistical analysis of corpus frequency data (significance tests in corpus linguistics, statistical association measures, Zipf's law and word frequency distributions), quantitative approaches to lexical semantics (collocations, multiword expressions and DSM), as well as processing large text corpora (IMS Open Corpus Workbench, data model and query language of the Nite XML Toolkit, tools for the Web as corpus). Stefan Evert has published extensively on collocations and association measures, has co-organised several workshops on multiword expressions as well as the ESSLLI 2008 workshop on distributional lexical semantics, and has co-taught an advanced course on DSM at ESSLLI 2009 with Alessandro Lenci, as well as a course on Computational Lexical Semantics with Gemma Boleda. The main focus of his current research is on understanding and improving DSMs for applications in natural language processing and lexical semantics.

URLS

[1] http://clic.cimec.unitn.it/marco/beyond_words/
[2] http://wordspace.collocations.de/doku.php/esslli:start
[3] http://art.uniroma2.it/gems/
[4] http://www.let.rug.nl/disco2009/
[5] http://sites.google.com/site/compneurowsnaacl10/
[6] http://art.uniroma2.it/gems010/
[7] http://clic.cimec.unitn.it/roberto/ESSLLI10-dsm-workshop/
[8] http://www.R-project.org/
[9] http://wordspace.collocations.de/doku.php/course:schedule

REFERENCES

Landauer, Thomas K. and Dumais, Susan T. (1997). A solution to Plato's problem: The latent semantic analysis theory of acquisition, induction and representation of knowledge. Psychological Review, 104(2), 211-240.

Lin, Dekang (1998). Automatic retrieval and clustering of similar words. In Proceedings of the 17th International Conference on Computational Linguistics (COLING-ACL 1998), pages 768-774, Montreal, Canada.

Mitchell, Tom M.; Shinkareva, Svetlana V.; Carlson, Andrew; Chang, Kai-Min; Malave, Vicente L.; Mason, Robert A.; Just, Marcel Adam (2008). Predicting human brain activity associated with the meanings of nouns. Science, 320, 1191-1195.

Murphy, Brian; Baroni, Marco; Poesio, Massimo (2009). EEG responds to conceptual stimuli and corpus semantics. In Proceedings of the 2009 Conference on Empirical Methods in Natural Language Processing, pages 619-627, Singapore.

Pantel, Patrick; Lin, Dekang (2000). An unsupervised approach to prepositional phrase attachment using contextually similar words. In Proceedings of the 38th Annual Meeting of the Association for Computational Linguistics, Hongkong, China.

Rapp, Reinhard (1999). Automatic identification of word translations from unrelated English and German corpora. In Proceedings of the 37th Annual Meeting of the Association for Computational Linguistics, Maryland.

Rapp, Reinhard (2004). A freely available automatically generated thesaurus of related words. In Proceedings of the 4th International Conference on Language Resources and Evaluation (LREC 2004), pages 395-398.

Schütze, Hinrich (1995). Distributional part-of-speech tagging. In Proceedings of the 7th Conference of the European Chapter of the Association for Computational Linguistics (EACL 1995), pages 141-148.

Schütze, Hinrich (1998). Automatic word sense discrimination. Computational Linguistics, 24(1), 97-123.

Turney, Peter D. (2006). Similarity of semantic relations. Computational Linguistics, 32 (3), 379-416.

Versley, Yannick (2008). Decorrelation and shallow semantic patterns for distributional clustering of nouns and verbs. In Proceedings of the ESSLLI Workshop on Distributional Lexical Semantics, pages 55-62, Hamburg, Germany.

Computational psycholinguistics

Roger Levy, Klinton Bicknell, and Nathaniel Smith
University of California, San Diego

1. Brief Description

Over the last two decades, computational linguistics has been revolutionized as a result of three closely related developments, two empirical and one theoretical: increases in computing power, the new availability of large linguistic datasets, and a paradigm shift toward the view that language processing by computers is best approached through the tools of statistical inference. During roughly the same time frame, there have been similar theoretical developments in cognitive psychology towards a view of major aspects of human cognition as instances of rational statistical inference. Developments in these two fields have set the stage for renewed interest in computational approaches to human language processing. In this tutorial, we briefly survey some of the key theoretical issues at the forefront of this interdisciplinary field today, and show how modeling techniques from NLP are being employed, extended, and coupled with experimental techniques from psycholinguistics to further our understanding of real-time human language use.

2. Tutorial structure

1. Introduction & summary of current state of key areas in psycholinguistics

(a) Key empirical findings involving ambiguity resolution, prediction, integration of diverse information sources, and speaker choice in real-time language comprehension and production (~10 minutes)
(b) Framing of empirical findings and concomitant theoretical issues in terms that can be cleanly related to leading NLP models and algorithms (~10 minutes)

2. Review of exact inference techniques for stochastic grammatical formalisms

(a) Weighted finite-state automata and context-free grammars (~10 minutes)
(b) Probabilistic Earley algorithm (~10 minutes)
(c) Weighted intersection of FSA and CFG (~10 minutes)

3. Modeling key results in ambiguity resolution and expectation-based facilitation

(a) Global disambiguation preferences (~5 minutes)
(b) Measuring online processing difficulty: intro to self-paced reading (~5 minutes)
(c) Expectation-based facilitation in unambiguous contexts (~5–10 minutes)

4. Coffee break

5. Online production: speaker choice

(a) Zipf's second law (frequency & word length) and information-theoretic interpretations (~10 minutes)
(b) Phonetic duration & reduction effects in online word production (~5 minutes)
(c) Morphological- and lexical-level reduction phenomena: modeling and empirical investigation (~10 minutes)

6. Cognitive limitations and implications for modeling

(a) Memory limitations & garden pathing: empirical results (~10 minutes)
(b) Modeling approach I: incremental beam search & garden pathing (~5 minutes)
(c) Modeling approach II: stochastic incremental search & "digging-in" effects (~10 minutes)

7. Additional theoretical challenges

(a) Bounds on rationality in real-time language use? "Good-enough" comprehension effects and "local-coherence" effects (~10 minutes)
(b) Possible avenues of attack: more refined models introducing input uncertainty (~10 minutes)
(c) More sophisticated experimental tools: eye-tracking (~5 minutes)
(d) New experimental findings on input uncertainty, "hallucinated" garden paths (~5 minutes)
(e) Future directions (~5 minutes)

8. Summary and questions (~5–10 minutes)

3. Instructor

Roger Levy, rlevy@ling.ucsd.edu

My research focuses on theoretical and applied questions in the processing of natural language. Inherently, linguistic communication involves the resolution of uncertainty over a potentially unbounded set of possible signals and meanings. How can a fixed set of knowledge and resources be deployed to manage this uncertainty? To address these questions I use a combination of computational modelling and psycholinguistic experimentation. This work furthers our understanding of the cognitive underpinning of language processing, and helps us design models and algorithms that will allow machines to process human language.

Klinton Bicknell and Nathaniel Smith are PhD students at the University of California, San Diego.

Textual Entailment

Mark Sammons, University of Illinois
Idan Szpektor, Yahoo!
V.G. Vinod Vydiswaran, University of Illinois

The NLP and ML communities are rising to grander, larger-scale challenges such as Machine Reading, Learning by Reading, and Learning to Read, challenges requiring deeper and more integrated natural language understanding capabilities.

The task of Recognizing Textual Entailment (RTE) requires automated systems to identify when two spans of text share a common meaning -- for example, that ``Alphaville Inc.'s attempted acquisition of Bauhaus led to a jump in both companies' stock prices" entails ``Bauahaus' stock rose", but not ``Alphaville acquired Bauhaus". This general capability would be a solid proxy for Natural Language Understanding, and has direct relevance to the grand challenges named above. Moreover, it could be used to improve performance in a large range of Natural Language Processing tasks such as Information Extraction, Question Answering, Exhaustive Search, Machine Translation and many others. The operational definition of Textual Entailment used by researchers in the field avoids commitment to any specific knowledge representation, inference method, or learning approach, thus encouraging application of a wide range of techniques to the problem.

Techniques developed for RTE have now been successfully applied in the domains of Question Answering, Relation Extraction, and Machine translation, and RTE systems continue to improve their performance even as the corpora on which they are evaluated (provided first by PASCAL, and now by NIST TAC) have become progressively more challenging. Over the sequence of RTE challenges from PASCAL and NIST TAC, the more successful systems seem to have converged in their overall approach.

The goal of this tutorial is to introduce the task of Recognizing Textual Entailment to researchers from other areas of NLP. We will identify and analyze common inference and learning approaches from a range of the more successful RTE systems, and investigate the role of knowledge resources. We will examine successful applications of RTE techniques to Question Answering and Machine Translation, and identify key research challenges that must be overcome to continue improving RTE systems.

Tutorial Outline

1. Introduction (35 minutes)

Define and motivate the Recognizing Textual Entailment (RTE) task. Introduce the RTE evaluation framework. Define the relationship between RTE and other major NLP tasks. Identify (some of) the semantic challenges inherent in the RTE task, including the introduction of 'contradiction' as an entailment category. Describe the use of RTE components/techniques in Question Answering, Machine Translation, and Relation Extraction.

2. The State of the Art (35 minutes)

Outline the basic structure underlying RTE systems. With reference to recent publications on RTE: cover the range of preprocessing/analysis that may be used; define representations/data structures typically used; outline inference procedures and machine learning techniques. Identify challenging aspects of the RTE problem in the context of system successes and failures.

3. Machine Learning for Recognizing Textual Entailment (35 minutes)

Describe the challenges involved in applying machine learning techniques to the Textual Entailment problem. Describe in more detail the main approaches to inference, which explicitly or implicitly use the concept of alignment. Show how alignment fits into assumptions of semantic compositionality, how it facilitates machine learning approaches, and how it can accommodate phenomena-specific resources. Show how it can be used for contradiction detection.

4. Knowledge Acquisition and Application in Textual Entailment (35 minutes)

Establish the role of knowledge resources in Textual Entailment, and the consequent importance of Knowledge Acquisition. Identify knowledge resources currently used in RTE systems, and their limitations. Describe existing knowledge acquisition approaches, emphasizing the need for learning directional semantic relations. Define suitable representations and algorithms for using knowledge, including context-sensitive knowledge application. Discuss the problem of noisy data, and the prospects for new knowledge resources/new acquisition approaches.

5. Key Challenges for Recognizing Textual Entailment (15 minutes)

Identify the key challenges in improving textual entailment systems: more reliable inputs (when is a solved problem not solved), domain adaptation, missing knowledge, scaling up. The need for a common entailment infrastructure to promote resource sharing and development.

Biographical Information of the Presenters

Mark Sammons
University of Illinois
201 N. Goodwin Ave.
Urbana, IL 61801 USA
Phone: 1-217-265-6759
Email: mssammon@illinois.edu

Mark Sammons is a Principal Research Scientist working with the Cognitive Computation Group at the University of Illinois. His primary interests are in Natural Language Processing and Machine Learning, with a focus on integrating diverse information sources in the context of Textual Entailment. His work has focused on developing a Textual Entailment framework that can easily incorporate new resources; designing appropriate inference procedures for recognizing entailment; and identifying and developing automated approaches to recognize and represent implicit content in natural language text. Mark received his MSC in Computer Science from the University of Illinois in 2004, and his PhD in Mechanical Engineering from the University of Leeds, England, in 2000.

Idan Szpektor
Yahoo! Research, Building 30 Matam Park, Haifa 31905, ISRAEL.
Phone: + 972-74-7924666; Email: idan@yahoo-inc.com

Idan Szpektor is a Research Scientist at Yahoo! Research. His primary research interests are in natural language processing, machine learning and information retrieval. Idan recently submitted his PhD thesis at Bar-Ilan University where he worked on unsupervised acquisition and application of broad-coverage knowledge-bases for Textual Entailment. He has been a main organizer of the second PASCAL Recognizing Textual Entailment Challenge and an advisor for the third RTE Challenge. He served on the program committees of EMNLP and TextInfer and reviewed papers for ACL, COLING and EMNLP. Idan Szpektor received his M.Sc. from Tel-Aviv University in 2005, where he worked on unsupervised knowledge acquisition for Textual Entailment.

V.G.Vinod Vydiswaran
University of Illinois
201 N. Goodwin Ave.
Urbana, IL 61801 USA

Phone: 1-217-333-2584
Email: vgvinodv@illinois.edu

V.G.Vinod Vydiswaran is a 3rd year Ph.D. student in the Department of Computer Science at the University of Illinois at Urbana-Champaign. His research interests include text informatics, natural language processing, machine learning, and information extraction. His work has included developing a Textual Entailment system, and applying Textual Entailment to relation extraction and information retrieval. He received his Masters degree from Indian Institute of Technology Bombay, India in 2004, where he worked on Conditional models for Information Extraction. Later, he worked at Yahoo! Research & Development Center at Bangalore, India, on scaling Information Extraction technologies over the Web.

Author Index